TABLE
Of Contents

1. George Washington
2. Thomas Jefferson
3. Abraham Lincoln
4. Woodrow Wilson
5. Franklin D. Roosevelt
6. Harry S. Truman
7. John F. Kennedy
8. Lyndon B. Johnson
9. Barack Obama
10. Presidential Stamps/Exit Ticket

Text 1

Annotation Checklist

As you read the text, please annotate it using the following checklist:

- ☑ Underline any main ideas
- ☑ Circle any words you don't know
- ☑ Look up the words online
- ☑ Reread anything you don't understand
- ☑ Summarize after rereading
- ☑ Write Down things you find interesting

yes!

Note Taking

Name: _____

Date: _____

George Washington: The First President of the United States

Have you ever thought about who became the very first President of the United States? That honor belongs to George Washington! He was known as the "Father of His Country" even when he was alive. Let's learn more about his life, struggles, and major achievements.

Early Life

George Washington was born on February 22, 1732, in Westmoreland County, Virginia. He grew up with a lot of siblings, having two older half-brothers, three brothers, and one sister. Sadly, his dad died when he was only 11 years old. Because of that, he couldn't go to school in England like his older brothers. Instead, he learned math, reading, and writing at a school near his home.

From a young age, George was taught to be a gentleman. That meant he needed to have good manners, tell the truth, and protect the weak. These lessons helped shape the great leader he would become.

Military Life

Before he became president, Washington was a soldier. He joined the military and fought in a war called the French and Indian War. He showed such bravery during battles that he became a hero to many people. But war was tough. He faced harsh winters, sickness, and sometimes didn't even have enough food for his soldiers.

Revolutionary War and Struggles
Later, when the American colonies decided they didn't want to be ruled by Britain anymore, Washington became the leader of the American army in the Revolutionary War. It wasn't easy! His army was smaller and had fewer guns and soldiers than the British army. They faced real struggles. There were times they were so cold they didn't have shoes and had to walk over ice and snow. But Washington never gave up.

One of the most famous moments was when Washington led his troops across the icy Delaware River on the night of December 25, 1776. They launched a surprise attack and won a huge victory!

Becoming the President
After the war, everyone knew Washington was a strong leader. So, when the United States needed its first president, they chose him! He was elected in 1789. Did you know he's the only president to have gotten all the votes from the electoral college? That means every person who could vote wanted him to be president!

As president, he had to make a lot of hard decisions. One of them was setting up the first bank of the United States to keep the country's money safe. He also made sure the U.S. Constitution was followed, setting up courts and making laws that still impact us today.

Life After Being President
After serving two terms (which means two times as president), Washington decided he didn't want to be president anymore. He retired to his home in Mount Vernon, Virginia. He really loved his farm and wanted to spend his days there. Unfortunately, he didn't get to enjoy his retirement for long. He died on December 14, 1799, from a throat infection.

Why Remember Washington?
George Washington showed everyone what it meant to be a good leader. Even though he could have been president for much longer, he chose to step down because he believed in something called "civic virtue" – that meant he thought more about what was good for everyone in the country than what was good for him alone.

Today, we remember him as a brave, wise, and fair leader. His face is on the U.S. dollar bill and quarter, and there's a very famous monument in Washington D.C., the Washington Monument, built just for him!

George Washington's life teaches us about bravery, leadership, and thinking about others. He helped shape the United States into the country it is today, and that's why we continue to honor him.

1. Which statement from the text best supports the fact that George Washington faced many hardships during war times?
    - a) "He grew up with a lot of siblings, having two older half-brothers, three brothers, and one sister."
    - b) "But war was tough. He faced harsh winters, sickness, and sometimes didn't even have enough food for his soldiers."
    - c) "He really loved his farm and wanted to spend his days there."
    - d) "They launched a surprise attack and won a huge victory!"
2. What is the main idea of this text?
    - a) The difficulties of war during the 18th century.
    - b) The life, challenges, and achievements of George Washington.
    - c) The process of becoming the President of the United States.
    - d) The reasons why George Washington is on the U.S. dollar bill.
3. Which detail from the text best supports the main idea that George Washington was a dedicated leader?
    - a) "George Washington was born on February 22, 1732, in Westmoreland County, Virginia."
    - b) "Instead, he learned math, reading, and writing at a school near his home."
    - c) "But Washington never gave up."
    - d) "He retired to his home in Mount Vernon, Virginia."
4. What does the term "civic virtue" most likely mean in the context of the passage?
    - a) Desire for power
    - b) Selfishness
    - c) Thinking about personal benefit
    - d) Considering the common good
5. How does the author present George Washington's character in this text?
    - a) As a flawed leader with many personal issues
    - b) As a brave and wise leader who thought about the greater good
    - c) As a leader who was mostly interested in financial gain
    - d) As someone who accidentally became a leader

6. Describe how the author's account of George Washington's crossing of the Delaware River contributes to our perception of him as a leader.

_____
_____
_____
_____

7. Explain how George Washington demonstrated "civic virtue" after his presidency, according to the text.

_____
_____
_____
_____

8. Using evidence from the text, explain how George Washington's early life prepared him for his future role as a leader.

_____
_____
_____
_____

Write an informative essay about the challenges George Washington faced during his military career and presidency and how these experiences shaped his legacy. Be sure to use evidence from the text to support your points.

_____
_____
_____
_____
_____
_____
_____
_____
_____
_____
_____
_____
_____
_____
_____
_____
_____

Answer key

1. Which statement from the text best supports the fact that George Washington faced many hardships during war times?
    - a) "He grew up with a lot of siblings, having two older half-brothers, three brothers, and one sister."
    - b) "But war was tough. He faced harsh winters, sickness, and sometimes didn't even have enough food for his soldiers."
    - c) "He really loved his farm and wanted to spend his days there."
    - d) "They launched a surprise attack and won a huge victory!"
2. What is the main idea of this text?
    - a) The difficulties of war during the 18th century.
    - b) The life, challenges, and achievements of George Washington.
    - c) The process of becoming the President of the United States.
    - d) The reasons why George Washington is on the U.S. dollar bill.
3. Which detail from the text best supports the main idea that George Washington was a dedicated leader?
    - a) "George Washington was born on February 22, 1732, in Westmoreland County, Virginia."
    - b) "Instead, he learned math, reading, and writing at a school near his home."
    - c) "But Washington never gave up."
    - d) "He retired to his home in Mount Vernon, Virginia."
4. What does the term "civic virtue" most likely mean in the context of the passage?
    - a) Desire for power
    - b) Selfishness
    - c) Thinking about personal benefit
    - d) Considering the common good
5. How does the author present George Washington's character in this text?
    - a) As a flawed leader with many personal issues
    - b) As a brave and wise leader who thought about the greater good
    - c) As a leader who was mostly interested in financial gain
    - d) As someone who accidentally became a leader

Text 2

Annotation Checklist

As you read the text, please annotate it using the following checklist:

- ☑ Underline any main ideas
- ☑ Circle any words you don't know
- ☑ Look up the words online
- ☑ Reread anything you don't understand
- ☑ Summarize after rereading
- ☑ Write Down things you find interesting

yes!

Note Taking

Name: _____

Date: _____

Thomas Jefferson: The Writer of Freedom

Did you know the United States has a special document that talks about freedom and rights? It's called the Declaration of Independence. The main person who wrote it was Thomas Jefferson. He did a lot more than just that! Let's learn about his life, his challenges, and the big things he did for our country.

Early Days
Thomas Jefferson was born on April 13, 1743, in Virginia. He lived in a big house on a place called Shadwell. When he was little, he loved reading books. By the time he was grown-up, he had read thousands of them! His family owned a lot of land, and they had many people working for them, including slaves. Slaves were Africans that were captured and made to work for free. It was harsh, cruel, and it was not right. But back than, unfortunately, this was common practice.

Declaration of Independence
When Jefferson was 33 years old, he did something super important. The American colonies were having problems with England. They wanted to be free and have their own country. Jefferson was chosen to write a letter to explain why. This letter was the Declaration of Independence. It said that all people are created equal and have rights that can't be taken away. This was a bold and brave thing to say back then!

Becoming President
After the United States became its own country, Thomas Jefferson wanted to help it grow and be strong. He became the third president of the United States in 1801. As president, he made some big decisions.

One of the coolest things he did was the Louisiana Purchase in 1803. He bought land from France that doubled the size of the U.S.! This land was so big that people didn't even know what was all there. So, he sent explorers Lewis and Clark to find out and make maps.

Struggles and Challenges
Being president is a tough job, and Jefferson had his own problems to deal with. Many people didn't agree with him, and they argued a lot. He worried about the United States being friends with other countries and wanted to make sure the U.S. stayed peaceful.

Also, even though Jefferson said all people are created equal, he owned slaves. This is something many people today find confusing and sad. It's important to remember that even great leaders can have things they don't do right.

After Being President
Jefferson only stayed president for two terms, which is eight years in total. After that, he went back to his home in Virginia, a beautiful place called Monticello. He designed this house himself! It sat on a big hill, and he could look out and see for miles.

Even though he wasn't president anymore, he still wanted to help people learn. He started a university called the University of Virginia. It's still around today!

Remembering Jefferson
Thomas Jefferson died on July 4, 1826, which is interesting because it's the same day the Declaration of Independence was approved. He was 83 years old.

Today, we remember him for many reasons. He believed in freedom and the rights of people. He also believed in the power of learning and reading. If you ever see a nickel or a two-dollar bill, you'll see Jefferson's face. There's also a big statue of him in Washington D.C., called the Jefferson Memorial.

Even though he wasn't perfect, Thomas Jefferson did a lot to help the United States grow. We can learn from both his successes and his mistakes. By understanding his story, we can better understand the story of America.

1. According to the text, why is Thomas Jefferson a significant figure in American history?
    - a) He was the richest president of the United States.
    - b) He wrote the Declaration of Independence and made substantial contributions as president.
    - c) He was the first person to explore the Louisiana territory.
    - d) He established the first bank in the United States.
2. What is the main idea of the text?
    - a) The challenges of presidency during the early days of the United States.
    - b) The life, accomplishments, and paradoxes of Thomas Jefferson.
    - c) The process of drafting the Declaration of Independence.
    - d) The expansion of the United States through land purchases.
3. Which detail from the text best supports the main idea that Thomas Jefferson had a lasting impact on education?
    - a) "When he was little, he loved reading books."
    - b) "So, he sent explorers Lewis and Clark to find out and make maps."
    - c) "He started a university called the University of Virginia."
    - d) "There's also a big statue of him in Washington D.C., called the Jefferson Memorial."
4. In the context of this text, what does the phrase "all people are created equal" most closely mean?
    - a) Every person deserves the same status and rights.
    - b) All people should have the same job opportunities.
    - c) Everyone needs to have equal wealth.
    - d) All citizens should vote in the elections.
5. How does the author illustrate Thomas Jefferson's character in this text?
    - a) As a perfect leader who made no mistakes.
    - b) As a proponent of freedom and education, with personal contradictions.
    - c) As a president who avoided all forms of conflict.
    - d) As someone primarily interested in architectural design.

6. How does the author's description of Jefferson's actions after his presidency contribute to our understanding of his character and values?

_____
_____
_____
_____

7. What were some contradictions in Thomas Jefferson's beliefs and actions, as presented in the text? How does acknowledging these contradictions help us understand his legacy?

_____
_____
_____
_____

8. Provide evidence from the text to explain how Thomas Jefferson's early interests and environment might have influenced his later achievements and values.

_____
_____
_____
_____

Compose an informative essay discussing the complexities of Thomas Jefferson's presidency, including both his achievements and the challenges he faced. Use evidence from the text to support your discussion.

Answer key

1. According to the text, why is Thomas Jefferson a significant figure in American history?
    - a) He was the richest president of the United States.
    - <u>b) He wrote the Declaration of Independence and made substantial contributions as president.</u>
    - c) He was the first person to explore the Louisiana territory.
    - d) He established the first bank in the United States.
2. What is the main idea of the text?
    - a) The challenges of presidency during the early days of the United States.
    - <u>b) The life, accomplishments, and paradoxes of Thomas Jefferson.</u>
    - c) The process of drafting the Declaration of Independence.
    - d) The expansion of the United States through land purchases.
3. Which detail from the text best supports the main idea that Thomas Jefferson had a lasting impact on education?
    - a) "When he was little, he loved reading books."
    - b) "So, he sent explorers Lewis and Clark to find out and make maps."
    - <u>c) "He started a university called the University of Virginia."</u>
    - d) "There's also a big statue of him in Washington D.C., called the Jefferson Memorial."
4. In the context of this text, what does the phrase "all people are created equal" most closely mean?
    - <u>a) Every person deserves the same status and rights.</u>
    - b) All people should have the same job opportunities.
    - c) Everyone needs to have equal wealth.
    - d) All citizens should vote in the elections.
5. How does the author illustrate Thomas Jefferson's character in this text?
    - a) As a perfect leader who made no mistakes.
    - <u>b) As a proponent of freedom and education, with personal contradictions.</u>
    - c) As a president who avoided all forms of conflict.
    - d) As someone primarily interested in architectural design.

Text 3

Annotation Checklist

As you read the text, please annotate it using the following checklist:

- [x] Underline any main ideas
- [x] Circle any words you don't know
- [x] Look up the words online
- [x] Reread anything you don't understand
- [x] Summarize after rereading
- [x] Write Down things you find interesting

Note Taking

Name: _____

Date: _____

Abraham Lincoln: From Log Cabin to the White House

Imagine growing up in a small log cabin in the countryside, then one day becoming the President of the United States! That's the incredible story of Abraham Lincoln, one of the most famous leaders in American history. Let's dive into his life, his big struggles, and the amazing things he did for America.

Humble Beginnings
Abraham Lincoln was born on February 12, 1809, in a log cabin in Kentucky. He didn't grow up with a lot of money or fancy things. His family moved to Indiana, and then to Illinois. When he was just nine years old, his mother died, which was very sad for him. Lincoln didn't go to school for long, but he loved to read. Any book he could get, he would read by the light of the fireplace.

Becoming Honest Abe
Lincoln worked many jobs before he became president. He was a store clerk, a surveyor who measured land, and a postmaster who looked after the mail. He was also a lawyer. People started calling him "Honest Abe" because he always told the truth, even when it was hard.

The Road to Presidency

Lincoln decided he wanted to help make laws, so he went into politics. In 1860, he ran for president and won! This was a very hard time for America. The country was divided over many things, one of which was slavery — the owning of people as property. Some states wanted to keep slavery, and others wanted to end it.

Civil War and Emancipation

Not long after Lincoln became president, something called the Civil War started in 1861. This was a war between the states that were part of the United States. It was brother against brother, and it was very, very sad.

One big thing Lincoln believed was that no one should be a slave. So, in 1863, he wrote the Emancipation Proclamation. This was a special order that said all slaves in places fighting against the United States were free. This didn't end slavery everywhere, but it was a big step.

Tough Times and Great Speeches

President Lincoln had to make many tough choices during the war. He was a good man but had a lot of sadness in his life. He lost two of his sons when they were little boys, and the war made him very sad, too. But he never gave up.

He gave famous speeches that people still remember today. One is called the Gettysburg Address. In this speech, he talked about how important it was for the country to be united and for everyone to be free.

The End of a Life, But Not a Legacy
Sadly, President Lincoln's story doesn't have a happy ending. Just after the Civil War ended in 1865, he went to a play at Ford's Theatre and was hurt by a man named John Wilkes Booth. President Lincoln died the next day. The whole country was very sad to lose him.

Remembering Lincoln Today
Even though Abraham Lincoln's life ended in sadness, his story is not a sad one. He worked his whole life to unite the country and to make sure all people were free. He's remembered as one of the greatest presidents of the United States.

You can see Lincoln's face on the penny and the five-dollar bill. In Washington D.C., there's a big statue of him sitting in a chair, the Lincoln Memorial, to honor all the great things he did.

Abraham Lincoln's life shows us that no matter where you start, you can make a difference. He teaches us about honesty, working hard, and caring for others. His story is a big part of America's story.

1. What was one reason Abraham Lincoln is remembered as an honest leader?
    - a) He freed all the slaves as soon as he became president.
    - b) He always told the truth, earning him the nickname "Honest Abe."
    - c) He won the Civil War single-handedly.
    - d) He wrote the Gettysburg Address before becoming president.
2. What is the main idea of this text?
    - a) The Civil War was the most significant war in American history.
    - b) The process by which the Emancipation Proclamation was written.
    - c) Abraham Lincoln's journey from humble beginnings to becoming a president who faced great challenges and made impactful decisions.
    - d) The assassination of famous figures in American history.
3. Which detail from the text best supports the main idea that Abraham Lincoln faced personal and professional challenges during his presidency?
    - a) "Lincoln didn't go to school for long, but he loved to read."
    - b) "He lost two of his sons when they were little boys, and the war made him very sad, too."
    - c) "He was a store clerk, a surveyor who measured land, and a postmaster who looked after the mail."
    - d) "In Washington D.C., there's a big statue of him sitting in a chair, the Lincoln Memorial."
4. What does the term "Emancipation Proclamation" refer to in the text?
    - a) A speech given by Lincoln during the Civil War.
    - b) A special order declaring the freedom of all slaves in places fighting against the United States.
    - c) The end of the Civil War.
    - d) Lincoln's decision to run for presidency.

5. Which statement best describes the author's viewpoint of Abraham Lincoln?
    - a) Lincoln was a perfect individual with no flaws.
    - b) Lincoln was a poor leader who made numerous mistakes.
    - c) Lincoln was a determined leader who faced personal loss and national turmoil with honesty and a commitment to unity and freedom.
    - d) Lincoln was primarily concerned with his own image and power.

6. How does the author's portrayal of Lincoln's personal tragedies deepen our understanding of his character and resilience?

_____
_____
_____
_____

7. How did Lincoln's actions during his presidency demonstrate his beliefs and values, according to the text? Please provide examples.

_____
_____
_____
_____

8. Using evidence from the text, describe how Abraham Lincoln's early life and career shaped his principles and actions as president.

_____
_____
_____
_____

Write an essay explaining how Abraham Lincoln's leadership qualities and decisions impacted the United States during and after his presidency. Use specific details from the text to support your discussion.

_____
_____
_____
_____
_____
_____
_____
_____
_____
_____
_____
_____
_____
_____
_____
_____
_____
_____

Answer key

1. What was one reason Abraham Lincoln is remembered as an honest leader?
    - a) He freed all the slaves as soon as he became president.
    - <u>b) He always told the truth, earning him the nickname "Honest Abe."</u>
    - c) He won the Civil War single-handedly.
    - d) He wrote the Gettysburg Address before becoming president.
2. What is the main idea of this text?
    - a) The Civil War was the most significant war in American history.
    - b) The process by which the Emancipation Proclamation was written.
    - <u>c) Abraham Lincoln's journey from humble beginnings to becoming a president who faced great challenges and made impactful decisions.</u>
    - d) The assassination of famous figures in American history.
3. Which detail from the text best supports the main idea that Abraham Lincoln faced personal and professional challenges during his presidency?
    - a) "Lincoln didn't go to school for long, but he loved to read."
    - <u>b) "He lost two of his sons when they were little boys, and the war made him very sad, too."</u>
    - c) "He was a store clerk, a surveyor who measured land, and a postmaster who looked after the mail."
    - d) "In Washington D.C., there's a big statue of him sitting in a chair, the Lincoln Memorial."
4. What does the term "Emancipation Proclamation" refer to in the text?
    - a) A speech given by Lincoln during the Civil War.
    - <u>b) A special order declaring the freedom of all slaves in places fighting against the United States.</u>
    - c) The end of the Civil War.
    - d) Lincoln's decision to run for presidency.

5. Which statement best describes the author's viewpoint of Abraham Lincoln?
    - a) Lincoln was a perfect individual with no flaws.
    - b) Lincoln was a poor leader who made numerous mistakes.
    - <u>c) Lincoln was a determined leader who faced personal loss and national turmoil with honesty and a commitment to unity and freedom.</u>
    - d) Lincoln was primarily concerned with his own image and power.

Text 4

Annotation Checklist

As you read the text, please annotate it using the following checklist:

- ☑ Underline any main ideas
- ☑ Circle any words you don't know
- ☑ Look up the words online
- ☑ Reread anything you don't understand
- ☑ Summarize after rereading
- ☑ Write Down things you find interesting

yes!

Note Taking

Name: _____

Date: _____

Woodrow Wilson: A President of Peace and Change

Can you imagine being the leader of a country during a world war? Woodrow Wilson, the 28th president of the United States, knew exactly how that felt. He was president during World War I, one of the biggest wars in history. But who was Woodrow Wilson, and how did he go from being a boy in the South during the Civil War to the President during World War I? Let's explore his life, the challenges he faced, and the changes he made that still affect us today.

Early Years and Education
Thomas Woodrow Wilson was born on December 28, 1856, in Staunton, Virginia. His dad was a minister, and his mom was a minister's daughter. He was born just before the Civil War, and he saw the effects of the war as he grew up, which was pretty intense for a young boy.

Wilson was a serious student and really loved to learn. He went to college at Princeton University, then studied law, and finally got a Ph.D. (that's the highest degree you can get!) in political science. He became a professor and then the president of Princeton University.

Into Politics
Even though Wilson had spent many years in education,

he was very interested in government and making changes in the country. So, he got into politics. He was elected the governor of New Jersey in 1910. As governor, he made many changes to the laws in New Jersey to make things fairer for everyone.

People across the country noticed the good things he was doing, and soon, he was elected President of the United States in 1912. He was the first president to hold a press conference, which is when the president talks to the news and they ask questions. He wanted to be honest and open with the people.

Big Changes for America
As president, Wilson made a lot of changes. He started the Federal Reserve System, which is how the government manages money. This was a big deal because it helped prevent things like economic downturns. Though, it is not a perfect system.

He also made laws that improved working conditions for people in factories and established the Federal Trade Commission, which keeps businesses from being unfair or lying about what they're selling. He wanted the people in America to have better lives and to be treated fairly at work.

World War I and Struggles for Peace
Something huge happened while Wilson was president: World War I. This was a very scary time because many countries were fighting, and lots of people were getting hurt. At first, Wilson didn't want America to join the war. He tried really hard to help the countries make peace. But in 1917, things got so bad that America had to join the war.

After the war, Wilson wanted to make sure a big war like that never happened again. He came up with a plan for peace called the Fourteen Points. The most important point was creating a group of countries that would work together to keep peace. This was the start of the League of Nations, which was like an early version of the United Nations we have today.

Sadly, even though the League of Nations was Wilson's idea, the United States didn't join. This was because the Senate didn't agree with Wilson, and they voted against joining. Wilson was very upset by this.

Hard Times and Later Years
The end of Wilson's time as president was tough. In 1919, he got very sick with a stroke, which made it hard for him to move and talk. His wife, Edith, helped him a lot with his presidential duties. He finished his second term as president, but he was too sick to run again.

Wilson retired and lived quietly until he died on February 3, 1924. He had worked hard his whole life to make the world a better, more peaceful place.

Wilson's Legacy
Today, we remember Woodrow Wilson for many reasons. He made big changes in the government and the economy that still affect us. He worked for peace during a really hard time in history. And even though not all his ideas worked out, he never stopped believing in a better world.

There's even a big award called the "Woodrow Wilson Award" that's given to people who work hard for public service, just like Wilson did.

Even though some of his views, especially on race and segregation, are seen as wrong today, learning about Wilson is important. We can celebrate the good things he did while also remembering the bad and thinking about how we can do better in the future.

Wilson's story teaches us that the world can change, even during tough times. It's a reminder that working hard and believing in good ideas can make a big difference, even if it's not always easy.

1. Why is Woodrow Wilson remembered today, despite some of his views now seen as wrong?
    - a) He was the president of Princeton University.
    - b) He made significant changes in government, worked for peace, and believed in a better world.
    - c) He was born in Virginia before the Civil War.
    - d) He suffered a stroke while in office.
2. What is the main idea of this text?
    - a) The causes and effects of World War I.
    - b) The establishment and functions of the Federal Reserve System.
    - c) Woodrow Wilson's life from his education to his presidency, highlighting the reforms he initiated and his efforts for global peace.
    - d) The controversial legacy of prominent figures in American history.
3. Which detail from the text best supports the main idea that Woodrow Wilson was dedicated to fairness and peace?
    - a) "Wilson was a serious student and really loved to learn."
    - b) "He made many changes to the laws in New Jersey to make things fairer for everyone."
    - c) "In 1919, he got very sick with a stroke, which made it hard for him to move and talk."
    - d) "There's even a big award called the 'Woodrow Wilson Award.'"
4. In the context of this text, what did the "Fourteen Points" represent?
    - a) A set of laws Wilson established in New Jersey.
    - b) The reasons America joined World War I.
    - c) Wilson's plan for global peace and the proposal for the League of Nations.
    - d) The economic policies Wilson enacted as president.

5. Which statement best reflects the author's viewpoint of Woodrow Wilson?
    - a) Wilson's presidency was flawless and his decisions were universally celebrated.
    - b) Wilson was an inconsequential leader whose actions had little lasting impact.
    - c) Wilson was a visionary who faced personal and political challenges, striving for domestic reform and international peace, albeit with a complex legacy.
    - d) Wilson's primary goal during his presidency was to gain personal fame and recognition.

6. How does the author acknowledge and handle the complexities of Woodrow Wilson's legacy in the text?

_____
_____
_____
_____

7. What were some of the key reforms Woodrow Wilson made during his presidency, and why were they important, according to the text?

_____
_____
_____
_____

8. Cite specific examples from the text that demonstrate Woodrow Wilson's commitment to education and public service before his presidency.

_____
_____
_____
_____

Discuss the challenges Woodrow Wilson faced during his presidency and how his actions and beliefs have had a lasting impact on the United States and the world. Use evidence from the text to support your answer.

_____
_____
_____
_____
_____
_____
_____
_____
_____
_____
_____
_____
_____
_____
_____
_____
_____
_____
_____
_____

Answer key

1. Why is Woodrow Wilson remembered today, despite some of his views now seen as wrong?
    - a) He was the president of Princeton University.
    - b) He made significant changes in government, worked for peace, and believed in a better world.
    - c) He was born in Virginia before the Civil War.
    - d) He suffered a stroke while in office.
2. What is the main idea of this text?
    - a) The causes and effects of World War I.
    - b) The establishment and functions of the Federal Reserve System.
    - c) Woodrow Wilson's life from his education to his presidency, highlighting the reforms he initiated and his efforts for global peace.
    - d) The controversial legacy of prominent figures in American history.
3. Which detail from the text best supports the main idea that Woodrow Wilson was dedicated to fairness and peace?
    - a) "Wilson was a serious student and really loved to learn."
    - b) "He made many changes to the laws in New Jersey to make things fairer for everyone."
    - c) "In 1919, he got very sick with a stroke, which made it hard for him to move and talk."
    - d) "There's even a big award called the 'Woodrow Wilson Award.'"
4. In the context of this text, what did the "Fourteen Points" represent?
    - a) A set of laws Wilson established in New Jersey.
    - b) The reasons America joined World War I.
    - c) Wilson's plan for global peace and the proposal for the League of Nations.
    - d) The economic policies Wilson enacted as president.

5. Which statement best reflects the author's viewpoint of Woodrow Wilson?
    - a) Wilson's presidency was flawless and his decisions were universally celebrated.
    - b) Wilson was an inconsequential leader whose actions had little lasting impact.
    - <u>c) Wilson was a visionary who faced personal and political challenges, striving for domestic reform and international peace, albeit with a complex legacy.</u>
    - d) Wilson's primary goal during his presidency was to gain personal fame and recognition.

Text 5

Annotation Checklist

As you read the text, please annotate it using the following checklist:

- ☑ Underline any main ideas
- ☑ Circle any words you don't know
- ☑ Look up the words online
- ☑ Reread anything you don't understand
- ☑ Summarize after rereading
- ☑ Write Down things you find interesting

yes!

Note Taking

Name: _____

Date: _____

Franklin D. Roosevelt: Leading Through Hard Times

What if you had to lead a country during the hardest of times? Franklin D. Roosevelt, also known as FDR, did just that! He was the President during the Great Depression and World War II, two of the toughest times in American history. But who was FDR before he became the President, and how did he guide America through these challenges? Let's learn about his life, his struggles, and his big achievements.

Growing Up
Franklin Delano Roosevelt was born on January 30, 1882, in Hyde Park, New York. He grew up in a wealthy family, with a lovely home and lots of opportunities for education and fun. He loved the outdoors and activities like horseback riding, rowing, and tennis.

For college, FDR went to Harvard University and later studied law at Columbia University. Though he didn't finish his law degree, he soon found his true calling in politics, just like his fifth cousin, President Theodore Roosevelt.

Early Political Career
In 1910, FDR was elected to the New York State Senate. People liked him because he cared about ordinary folks and worked

hard for them. Later, he worked for the U.S. Navy and then ran for Vice President, but he didn't win. However, FDR's journey was just beginning!

Overcoming Personal Challenges
In 1921, something tough happened. FDR got a disease called polio, which made it so he couldn't move his legs. This was a huge challenge for him. But FDR was strong and determined. He never gave up his political dreams, even when he had to use a wheelchair.

His wife, Eleanor Roosevelt, helped him a lot. She became his partner in politics, meeting people and giving speeches when FDR couldn't. They were an unstoppable team!

Becoming President
In 1932, during the Great Depression (a time when money was tight, and many people couldn't find jobs), FDR was elected President. He promised the American people a "New Deal," and he sure did deliver! The New Deal was a bunch of programs to create jobs, help businesses, and improve the economy.

FDR started programs like the Civilian Conservation Corps (CCC) to create jobs and build parks, and the Social Security Act to help elderly people. He used the radio to talk to the people in "Fireside Chats," making them feel like he was right there in their living room with them!

Leading During War
Just when things were starting to get better from the Great Depression, World War II began. FDR had to lead the country during a really scary time. He worked with leaders from other countries like Winston Churchill from the United Kingdom and Joseph Stalin from the Soviet Union.

In 1941, after the attack on Pearl Harbor, America joined the war. FDR said that day would live in "infamy," which means being known for something bad. He promised to defend America and its freedoms.

Four Terms and a Lasting Legacy
FDR was the only President ever to be elected four times! That's because he was a leader during such critical moments in history, and the people trusted him. But being President for so long was hard work, and in 1945, just before World War II ended, FDR died. He had given so much of himself to the country.

Today, FDR is remembered for his courage, optimism, and strong leadership. He showed that having a disability doesn't stop someone from doing great things. He also created programs that people still use today, like Social Security.

Remembering FDR
There are many places you can visit to learn more about FDR. There's the Franklin D. Roosevelt Presidential Library and Museum in Hyde Park, New York. You can also see his face on the dime, and there's a memorial for him in Washington D.C.

FDR's story teaches us that we can overcome big challenges with determination, hard work, and a little bit of hope. He led the country through tough times with a steady hand and a belief that things could get better. And thanks to him, they did!

1. What is one reason Franklin D. Roosevelt is remembered today?
    - a) He was related to Theodore Roosevelt.
    - b) He won a vice-presidential campaign early in his career.
    - c) He led the country through the Great Depression and World War II with impactful programs and strong leadership.
    - d) He completed a law degree at Columbia University.
2. What is the main idea of this text?
    - a) The strategies used by the U.S. during World War II.
    - b) The life of FDR, highlighting his personal and political challenges and his leadership during critical moments in American history.
    - c) The political dynamics of the early 20th century in America.
    - d) The detailed policies included in the New Deal.
3. Which detail from the text best supports the main idea that FDR was a resilient and effective leader?
    - a) "FDR went to Harvard University and later studied law at Columbia University."
    - b) "He loved the outdoors and activities like horseback riding, rowing, and tennis."
    - c) "He worked with leaders from other countries like Winston Churchill from the United Kingdom and Joseph Stalin from the Soviet Union."
    - d) "FDR got a disease called polio, which made it so he couldn't move his legs."

4. In the context of this text, what does the term "infamy" mean?
    - a) A state of extreme happiness.
    - b) Being well-known for a bad event or action.
    - c) A significant military victory.
    - d) A moment of international cooperation.
5. Which statement best reflects the author's viewpoint of Franklin D. Roosevelt?
    - a) FDR's political career was marked by constant failures and setbacks.
    - b) FDR was a privileged individual who used his wealth for personal gain.
    - c) FDR was a courageous and determined leader who guided America through difficult periods with innovative programs and empathy.
    - d) FDR's presidency had little to no impact on American history.

6. How does the author convey a sense of admiration and respect for FDR in the text?

_____
_____
_____
_____

7. Explain how the "New Deal" programs highlighted in the text were intended to address the issues of the Great Depression.

_____
_____
_____
_____

8. Provide evidence from the text to show how FDR's personal challenges influenced his political career and leadership style.

_____
_____
_____
_____

Write an essay on how Franklin D. Roosevelt's leadership during the Great Depression and World War II shaped the future of America. Include details from the text about his policies, personal struggles, and the legacy he left behind.

_____
_____
_____
_____
_____
_____
_____
_____
_____
_____
_____
_____
_____
_____
_____
_____
_____
_____

Answer key

1. What is one reason Franklin D. Roosevelt is remembered today?
    - a) He was related to Theodore Roosevelt.
    - <u>b) He won a vice-presidential campaign early in his career.
    c) He led the country through the Great Depression and World War II with impactful programs and strong leadership.</u>
    - d) He completed a law degree at Columbia University.
2. What is the main idea of this text?
    - a) The strategies used by the U.S. during World War II.
    - <u>b) The life of FDR, highlighting his personal and political challenges and his leadership during critical moments in American history.</u>
    - c) The political dynamics of the early 20th century in America.
    - d) The detailed policies included in the New Deal.
3. Which detail from the text best supports the main idea that FDR was a resilient and effective leader?
    - a) "FDR went to Harvard University and later studied law at Columbia University."
    - b) "He loved the outdoors and activities like horseback riding, rowing, and tennis."
    - <u>c) "He worked with leaders from other countries like Winston Churchill from the United Kingdom and Joseph Stalin from the Soviet Union."</u>
    - d) "FDR got a disease called polio, which made it so he couldn't move his legs."

4. In the context of this text, what does the term "infamy" mean?
    - a) A state of extreme happiness.
    - <u>b) Being well-known for a bad event or action.</u>
    - c) A significant military victory.
    - d) A moment of international cooperation.
5. Which statement best reflects the author's viewpoint of Franklin D. Roosevelt?
    - a) FDR's political career was marked by constant failures and setbacks.
    - b) FDR was a privileged individual who used his wealth for personal gain.
    - <u>c) FDR was a courageous and determined leader who guided America through difficult periods with innovative programs and empathy.</u>
    - d) FDR's presidency had little to no impact on American history.

Text 6

Annotation Checklist

As you read the text, please annotate it using the following checklist:

- ☑ Underline any main ideas
- ☑ Circle any words you don't know
- ☑ Look up the words online
- ☑ Reread anything you don't understand
- ☑ Summarize after rereading
- ☑ Write Down things you find interesting

yes!

Note Taking

Name: _____

Date: _____

Harry S. Truman: The Decisive President

Imagine having to make some of the hardest decisions ever, like whether to end a world war! That was the reality for Harry S. Truman, the 33rd President of the United States. But how did a boy from Missouri become the man making decisions that affected the whole world? Let's discover his journey, his tough choices, and how he made a difference in history.

Missouri Roots
Harry S. Truman was born on May 8, 1884, in Lamar, Missouri. He was the oldest child, and his family lived on a farm. Life wasn't always easy, especially when the family lost the farm and moved to Independence, Missouri. Despite the challenges, Harry loved to read, especially history and music.

After high school, Harry had various jobs, including working on the railroad and in a bank. He didn't go straight to college like some other presidents. Instead, he served in the military during World War I, which was a big war in Europe. This experience made him a strong leader.

Entering Politics
After the war, Truman returned to Missouri and got into politics, with help from his war buddies and a powerful politician named Tom Pendergast. He became a county judge,

which was more like an administrator than a courtroom judge, and then a U.S. Senator. People liked him because he was straightforward and honest.

Becoming President
Truman became Vice President in 1944, under President Franklin D. Roosevelt. But when FDR died in April 1945, Truman had to step up and become President. He had been Vice President for only 82 days!

Suddenly, Truman had to make decisions about World War II, which was still going on. Imagine how much pressure that was!

Tough Decisions
When Truman became President in 1945 after Roosevelt's death, he faced monumental challenges. The world was still engulfed in war, and he was suddenly thrust into coordinating the final stages of World War II. His decision to use the atomic bomb against Japan was one of the most significant and controversial decisions in world history. Truman always maintained that his choice led to a quicker end to the war and saved countless lives, though it also began the nuclear age.

After the war, Truman had more work to do. He wanted to help Europe recover, so he started the Marshall Plan, giving billions of dollars to help rebuild the countries affected by the war. This showed America's support for peace and freedom in the world.

Fighting for Fairness

Truman believed in fairness. One of the bravest things he did was to fight for civil rights, which are rights for all people, no matter their race. He knew that African Americans were not being treated fairly in the United States, especially in the South.

In 1948, he ordered the end of racial segregation in the military. This meant that soldiers of all races could serve together. Some people didn't like this, but Truman knew it was the right thing to do.

The Korean War and Beyond

In 1950, another war started in Korea, a country in Asia. North Korea invaded South Korea, and Truman decided that America would help South Korea. This was the start of the Korean War. Truman didn't run for president again after his term ended in 1953. He returned to Missouri and dedicated his time to creating his presidential library, where people could learn about American history and his presidency.

Remembering Truman

Harry S. Truman died on December 26, 1972, but his legacy lives on. He's remembered for his honesty, his tough decisions, and his dedication to peace and fairness.

Today, you can visit the Harry S. Truman Presidential Library and Museum in Independence, Missouri, to learn more about him. And guess what? He's the only president who had a library named after him and worked there!

Truman's life shows that even the boy from a small town in Missouri can grow up to be president. His story teaches us about bravery, making hard choices, and standing up for what's right, even when it's not easy.

1. What significant action did Harry S. Truman take that led to the end of World War II?
    - a) He initiated the Marshall Plan.
    - b) He ordered the end of racial segregation in the military.
    - c) He used the atomic bomb on two cities in Japan.
    - d) He served in the military during World War I.
2. What is the primary focus of this text?
    - a) The detailed events of World War II.
    - b) Harry S. Truman's life, including his rise to presidency and the difficult decisions he made in the interest of his country and peace.
    - c) The intricacies of the Korean War.
    - d) The process of establishing a presidential library.
3. In the context of this text, what does the term "segregation" mean?
    - a) Joining together of different groups.
    - b) Equal treatment for all people.
    - c) Keeping different racial groups separated.
    - d) Allocation of funds to different projects.
4. Which statement best reflects the author's viewpoint of Harry S. Truman?
    - a) Truman was indecisive and often avoided making tough choices.
    - b) Truman was a controversial figure who prioritized military actions over diplomatic solutions.
    - c) Truman was an honest, brave leader known for making hard choices and advocating for fairness and peace.
    - d) Truman's presidency was marked by numerous political scandals and conflicts.

1. What significant action did Harry S. Truman take that led to the end of World War II?
    - a) He initiated the Marshall Plan.
    - b) He ordered the end of racial segregation in the military.
    - c) He used the atomic bomb on two cities in Japan.
    - d) He served in the military during World War I.
2. What is the primary focus of this text?
    - a) The detailed events of World War II.
    - b) Harry S. Truman's life, including his rise to presidency and the difficult decisions he made in the interest of his country and peace.
    - c) The intricacies of the Korean War.
    - d) The process of establishing a presidential library.
3. In the context of this text, what does the term "segregation" mean?
    - a) Joining together of different groups.
    - b) Equal treatment for all people.
    - c) Keeping different racial groups separated.
    - d) Allocation of funds to different projects.
4. Which statement best reflects the author's viewpoint of Harry S. Truman?
    - a) Truman was indecisive and often avoided making tough choices.
    - b) Truman was a controversial figure who prioritized military actions over diplomatic solutions.
    - c) Truman was an honest, brave leader known for making hard choices and advocating for fairness and peace.
    - d) Truman's presidency was marked by numerous political scandals and conflicts.

5. Discuss the significant challenges Harry S. Truman faced during his presidency, and explain how he addressed each one. Include details from the text about his tough decisions and their impact on the nation and the world.

_____
_____
_____
_____

6. What evidence does the author provide to show Truman's commitment to fairness and civil rights?

_____
_____
_____
_____

7. Based on the text, what characteristics or values did Truman prioritize during his presidency?

_____
_____
_____
_____

Write an essay on how Harry S. Truman's presidency was marked by tough decisions, highlighting how these decisions impacted America and the world. Be sure to include information from the text about his early life, his approach to civil rights, and his strategies during times of war.

_____
_____
_____
_____
_____
_____
_____
_____
_____
_____
_____
_____
_____
_____
_____
_____
_____
_____
_____

Answer key

1 What significant action did Harry S. Truman take that led to the end of World War II?
- a) He initiated the Marshall Plan.
- b) He ordered the end of racial segregation in the military.
- <u>c) He used the atomic bomb on two cities in Japan.</u>
- d) He served in the military during World War I.

2. What is the primary focus of this text?
- a) The detailed events of World War II.
- <u>b) Harry S. Truman's life, including his rise to presidency and the difficult decisions he made in the interest of his country and peace.</u>
- c) The intricacies of the Korean War.
- d) The process of establishing a presidential library.

3. In the context of this text, what does the term "segregation" mean?
- a) Joining together of different groups.
- <u>b) Equal treatment for all people.</u>
- c) Keeping different racial groups separated.
- d) Allocation of funds to different projects.

4. Which statement best reflects the author's viewpoint of Harry S. Truman?
- a) Truman was indecisive and often avoided making tough choices.
- b) Truman was a controversial figure who prioritized military actions over diplomatic solutions.
- <u>c) Truman was an honest, brave leader known for making hard choices and advocating for fairness and peace.</u>
- d) Truman's presidency was marked by numerous political scandals and conflicts.

Text 7

Annotation Checklist

As you read the text, please annotate it using the following checklist:

- [x] Underline any main ideas
- [x] Circle any words you don't know
- [x] Look up the words online
- [x] Reread anything you don't understand
- [x] Summarize after rereading
- [x] Write Down things you find interesting

Note Taking

Note Taking

Name: _____

Date: _____

John F. Kennedy: The Young President Who Dreamed Big

A Boy from Boston

John Fitzgerald Kennedy, often called JFK, was born on May 29, 1917, in Brookline, Massachusetts. He was the second of nine kids in the Kennedy family, a well-known and wealthy family in Boston. JFK's parents always told their children about the importance of public service, which means helping your country and community.

Growing up, JFK faced health problems that often kept him in bed. But this didn't hold him back. While resting, he read many books and learned about history and politics. This sparked his dream of one day serving his country.

Education and War Service

JFK studied at Harvard University, one of the top schools in the country. There, he wrote a book about why England wasn't prepared for World War II, which became a bestseller. Soon after, JFK himself would experience the war.

During World War II, JFK served in the Navy. He became a hero when the boat he commanded, PT-109, was hit by an enemy ship. Even though he was injured, JFK bravely helped his crew to safety. This act of bravery became a famous story in his life.

Early Political Life

After the war, JFK decided to enter politics. He was first elected to the U.S. House of Representatives in 1947 and then to the Senate in 1953. He was known for his charm, intelligence, and excellent speeches. People loved to listen to him talk about his vision for America.

While serving as a senator, JFK faced more health challenges and had many surgeries. But he never gave up. He even wrote another book called "Profiles in Courage," which told the stories of brave people in American history. This book won a big prize called the Pulitzer Prize.

Becoming President

In 1960, JFK decided to run for President. He was young, and some people weren't sure if he was ready. But during a series of debates on TV, many Americans saw how smart and confident he was, especially against his opponent, Richard Nixon. JFK talked about a "New Frontier" for America, where science, civil rights, and peace would be priorities.

In a close election, JFK won and became the youngest person ever elected President. His beautiful wife, Jacqueline, and their two children, Caroline and John Jr., joined him in the White House.

Major Moments in JFK's Presidency

Being President in the 1960s was not easy. The world was changing fast, and America faced many challenges. Here are some of his biggest wins!

1. Space Race: JFK wanted America to be a leader in space exploration. He promised that by the end of the 1960s, an American astronaut would walk on the Moon. This dream came true in 1969.
2. Civil Rights: America was going through a big change as African Americans were fighting for equal rights. JFK supported them and made a famous speech where he said that every American should be treated the same, no matter their skin color.
3. Cuban Missile Crisis: In 1962, America and the Soviet Union almost had a nuclear war because of missiles in Cuba. It was a scary time, but JFK's strong leadership and smart decisions kept the peace.
4. Peace Corps: JFK believed that young Americans could help make the world a better place. He started the Peace Corps, where volunteers went to other countries to teach, build schools, and share their skills.

A Tragic End

JFK's time as President was cut short in a very sad way. On November 22, 1963, while he was in Dallas, Texas, JFK was shot and killed. The whole country was in shock and mourned the loss of their young President.

Though his time as President was short, JFK left a big mark on America. He inspired people to dream big and work hard for their country. His famous words, "Ask not what your country can do for you; ask what you can do for your country," encouraged Americans to be active and help their communities.

Legacy and Impact

JFK's impact on America and the world is still felt today. His push for space exploration led to many discoveries and technological advancements. His support for civil rights helped pave the way for equality. And his vision of peace and collaboration is remembered through programs like the Peace Corps.

There are many places you can visit to learn about JFK. The John F. Kennedy Presidential Library and Museum in Boston is a great place to explore his life and achievements.

A Lasting Memory

John F. Kennedy's story is one of hope, ambition, and service. From a young boy in Boston to the highest office in the land, he showed that with passion and determination, you can achieve great things. JFK's legacy reminds us that even in challenging times, we can dream big and work towards a better future.

1. What motivated JFK's interest in history and politics when he was young?
    - a) His family's political background.
    - b) His time at Harvard University.
    - c) His health problems that often kept him bedridden, leading him to read many books.
    - d) His service in World War II.
2. What is the primary message of the text about John F. Kennedy?
    - a) JFK's war service and bravery.
    - b) The challenges JFK faced during his presidency.
    - c) The journey of JFK from his youth to becoming a President who inspired a nation.
    - d) The family background and wealth of the Kennedys.
3. Which of the following did JFK establish to encourage young Americans to make the world a better place?
    - a) Civil Rights Act
    - b) NASA
    - c) Peace Corps
    - d) Harvard Youth Program
4. In the text, what does "public service" refer to?
    - a) Running for political office.
    - b) Helping your country and community.
    - c) Serving in the military.
    - d) Winning awards and recognition.
5. What perspective does the author convey regarding JFK's handling of the Cuban Missile Crisis?
    - a) JFK was unsure and indecisive during the crisis.
    - b) JFK made impulsive decisions that aggravated the situation.
    - c) JFK's leadership and smart decisions were critical in maintaining peace during the crisis.
    - d) JFK relied solely on others for decision-making.

6. How does the author depict JFK's commitment to the Civil Rights movement in America?

_____
_____
_____
_____

7. Provide evidence from the text that demonstrates JFK's dedication to global peace and collaboration.

_____
_____
_____
_____

8. Discuss the major challenges JFK faced during his presidency and describe how he addressed each of them, citing examples from the text.

_____
_____
_____
_____

Reflect on the legacy of John F. Kennedy. Using evidence from the text, explain how his visions, decisions, and programs have left a lasting impact on America and its place in the world.

_____
_____
_____
_____
_____
_____
_____
_____
_____
_____
_____
_____
_____
_____
_____
_____
_____
_____
_____
_____

Answer key

1. What motivated JFK's interest in history and politics when he was young?
    - a) His family's political background.
    - b) His time at Harvard University.
    - <u>c) His health problems that often kept him bedridden, leading him to read many books.</u>
    - d) His service in World War II.
2. What is the primary message of the text about John F. Kennedy?
    - a) JFK's war service and bravery.
    - b) The challenges JFK faced during his presidency.
    - <u>c) The journey of JFK from his youth to becoming a President who inspired a nation.</u>
    - d) The family background and wealth of the Kennedys.
3. Which of the following did JFK establish to encourage young Americans to make the world a better place?
    - a) Civil Rights Act
    - b) NASA
    - <u>c) Peace Corps</u>
    - d) Harvard Youth Program
4. In the text, what does "public service" refer to?
    - a) Running for political office.
    - <u>b) Helping your country and community.</u>
    - c) Serving in the military.
    - d) Winning awards and recognition.
5. What perspective does the author convey regarding JFK's handling of the Cuban Missile Crisis?
    - a) JFK was unsure and indecisive during the crisis.
    - b) JFK made impulsive decisions that aggravated the situation.
    - <u>c) JFK's leadership and smart decisions were critical in maintaining peace during the crisis.</u>
    - d) JFK relied solely on others for decision-making.

Text 8

Annotation Checklist

As you read the text, please annotate it using the following checklist:

- [x] Underline any main ideas
- [x] Circle any words you don't know
- [x] Look up the words online
- [x] Reread anything you don't understand
- [x] Summarize after rereading
- [x] Write Down things you find interesting

yes!

Note Taking

Name: _____

Date: _____

Lyndon B. Johnson: The Texan Who Transformed America

A Hill Country Beginning
Lyndon Baines Johnson, often known as LBJ, was born on August 27, 1908, in Stonewall, Texas. Growing up in the Texas Hill Country, Johnson's family faced financial hardships, teaching him the values of perseverance and hard work. These early experiences would shape his dedication to improving the lives of the less fortunate.

Teaching and Early Politics
Before stepping into the political arena, Johnson briefly worked as a school teacher. Teaching in a small Texas town, he observed the effects of poverty on his students, which deeply affected him. This experience ignited his passion for public service.

LBJ quickly transitioned to politics, serving first as a congressional aide and later as a U.S. Representative. His tall stature and charismatic personality made him hard to ignore. He was a master at building relationships, which helped him get things done in Washington.

The Senate and Vice Presidency
Johnson's political journey took a significant leap when he was elected to the U.S. Senate in 1948. Here, he became known

for his exceptional leadership skills, eventually becoming the Senate Majority Leader. LBJ had an uncanny ability to persuade and negotiate, which made him highly effective.

His political stature grew, leading him to become John F. Kennedy's Vice President after a close and contested election in 1960. Together, they aimed to bring progress and change to America.

Becoming President
LBJ's life took a dramatic turn on November 22, 1963. Following the tragic assassination of JFK in Dallas, Johnson was suddenly sworn in as the 36th President of the United States aboard Air Force One. It was a daunting task to lead a grieving nation, but LBJ was determined to honor Kennedy's legacy.

Sweeping Changes: The Great Society
One of Johnson's most significant contributions was his vision for a "Great Society," which aimed to eliminate poverty and racial injustice in America. Under this vision, several landmark pieces of legislation were passed:

- **Civil Rights:** LBJ signed the Civil Rights Act of 1964, which ended segregation in public places and banned employment discrimination based on race, color, religion, or national origin. He also signed the Voting Rights Act of 1965, ensuring African Americans the right to vote.

- **Education:** The Elementary and Secondary Education Act provided federal funding to schools, especially those in impoverished areas, to ensure every child had a fair chance at a quality education.
- **Healthcare:** Medicare and Medicaid were established, offering healthcare to the elderly and low-income individuals, respectively.
- **War on Poverty:** Several programs, like Head Start and Job Corps, were initiated to help people escape the cycle of poverty.

The Shadow of Vietnam

While Johnson achieved great success on the domestic front, his presidency was overshadowed by the Vietnam War. Initially inheriting the conflict from previous administrations, LBJ escalated American involvement. The war became deeply unpopular, leading to massive protests. The weight of the conflict and its controversies would become a defining aspect of his presidency.

Stepping Away

Facing criticism from both the war and divisions at home, LBJ surprised the nation in 1968 by announcing he would not seek re-election. This decision emphasized his commitment to peace negotiations in Vietnam over political ambition.

Final Years and Legacy

After leaving the presidency, LBJ returned to his Texas ranch, where he penned his memoirs and focused on the LBJ Library and School of Public Affairs at the University of Texas. He passed away on January 22, 1973.

Today, Lyndon B. Johnson's legacy is multifaceted. He's remembered for dramatically reshaping U.S. social policy, championing civil rights, and expanding the role of government in education and healthcare. Yet, his legacy is also intertwined with the Vietnam War's complexities and controversies.

A Larger-than-Life Texan
LBJ's life was a blend of immense accomplishments and challenging decisions. From the Texas hills to the White House corridors, Johnson showcased an unwavering commitment to public service. His ability to push for transformative policies has left an indelible mark on American society. LBJ's story is a testament to the power and challenges of leadership in turbulent times.

1. What was one of LBJ's motivations for public service?
    - a) He wanted to gain popularity.
    - b) He observed the effects of poverty on his students.
    - c) He was inspired by a famous author.
    - d) He wanted to travel the world.
2. What was the central theme of LBJ's vision for a "Great Society"?
    - a) Increase military strength.
    - b) Eliminate poverty and racial injustice.
    - c) Expand international relations.
    - d) Increase technological advancements.
3. Which of the following was NOT an initiative under LBJ's "Great Society"?
    - a) Medicare and Medicaid.
    - b) Space exploration.
    - c) The Civil Rights Act of 1964.
    - d) The Elementary and Secondary Education Act.
4. In the passage, the word "multifaceted" most likely means:
    - a) Simple.
    - b) With many sides or aspects.
    - c) Confusing.
    - d) Two-faced.
5. Which of the following best describes the author's perspective on LBJ's legacy?
    - a) It was solely positive with no controversies.
    - b) It was marred only by the Vietnam War.
    - c) It was a mix of accomplishments and challenges.
    - d) LBJ had no significant impact on America.

6. How did the author convey the contrast between LBJ's domestic achievements and the shadow of the Vietnam War on his presidency?

_____
_____
_____
_____

7. Using evidence from the text, explain how LBJ's early life experiences influenced his political agenda and priorities as President.

_____
_____
_____
_____

8. What major pieces of legislation or initiatives were launched under LBJ's vision of the "Great Society"?

_____
_____
_____
_____

Discuss the transformative impact of Lyndon B. Johnson's presidency on American society. Highlight the significant initiatives and reforms he introduced and explain how they have shaped the United States' socio-political landscape.

Answer key

1. What was one of LBJ's motivations for public service?
    - a) He wanted to gain popularity.
    - <u>b) He observed the effects of poverty on his students.</u>
    - c) He was inspired by a famous author.
    - d) He wanted to travel the world.
2. What was the central theme of LBJ's vision for a "Great Society"?
    - a) Increase military strength.
    - <u>b) Eliminate poverty and racial injustice.</u>
    - c) Expand international relations.
    - d) Increase technological advancements.
3. Which of the following was NOT an initiative under LBJ's "Great Society"?
    - a) Medicare and Medicaid.
    - <u>b) Space exploration.</u>
    - c) The Civil Rights Act of 1964.
    - d) The Elementary and Secondary Education Act.
4. In the passage, the word "multifaceted" most likely means:
    - a) Simple.
    - <u>b) With many sides or aspects.</u>
    - c) Confusing.
    - d) Two-faced.
5. Which of the following best describes the author's perspective on LBJ's legacy?
    - a) It was solely positive with no controversies.
    - b) It was marred only by the Vietnam War.
    - <u>c) It was a mix of accomplishments and challenges.</u>
    - d) LBJ had no significant impact on America.

Text 9

Annotation Checklist

As you read the text, please annotate it using the following checklist:

- ✅ Underline any main ideas
- ✅ Circle any words you don't know
- ✅ Look up the words online
- ✅ Reread anything you don't understand
- ✅ Summarize after rereading
- ✅ Write Down things you find interesting

Note Taking

Name: _____

Date: _____

Barack Obama: Breaking Barriers and Inspiring Change

Early Life and Dreams
Barack Hussein Obama was born on August 4, 1961, in Honolulu, Hawaii. With a Kenyan father and an American mother from Kansas, Barack's early life was a blend of cultures. His parents' union and eventual separation taught him the complexities of relationships and identities.

Growing up, Obama often felt the struggle of finding his place in the world, which he would later describe in his memoir, "Dreams from My Father." After high school, he moved to the mainland U.S. to study, first at Occidental College and later at Columbia University in New York.

Community Organizer to Lawmaker
After college, Obama moved to Chicago, where he became a community organizer. In this role, he helped people improve their lives, especially in neighborhoods that faced economic difficulties.

Driven by the desire to create larger change, Obama decided to study law. He attended Harvard Law School, where he achieved the significant honor of becoming the first African American president of the 'Harvard Law Review'.

Returning to Chicago, he taught law and continued community work. His journey into politics began in the Illinois State Senate, where he served from 1997 to 2004.

A National Spotlight and the Road to Presidency
Obama's national debut came during the 2004 Democratic National Convention. His speech about unity and the shared dreams of all Americans made him an instant star in the Democratic Party.

In 2008, after serving a short term in the U.S. Senate, Obama announced his run for the presidency. With messages of hope and change, he inspired many, especially the young and marginalized communities. After a historic campaign, Barack Obama was elected the 44th President of the United States, becoming the first African American to hold the office.

Key Moments of Obama's Presidency
- Healthcare Reform: One of his main achievements was the Affordable Care Act, commonly known as "Obamacare". This law aimed to make health insurance available to more Americans.
- Environmental Concerns: Obama believed in the threat of climate change. He signed agreements like the Paris Climate Accord, committing the U.S. to reduce carbon emissions.
- Relationships with Cuba: In a historic move, Obama reestablished diplomatic ties with Cuba after decades of tension.

Challenges and Controversies
Like all presidents, Obama faced challenges. He navigated the country through economic hardships following the 2008 financial crisis. His policies, especially in areas like healthcare and immigration, faced opposition and sparked national debates. Internationally, he dealt with complex issues in places like Syria, Russia, and North Korea.

Life After Presidency
After serving two terms, Obama stepped down in 2017. He didn't leave the public eye, though. Alongside his wife, Michelle, he established the Obama Foundation, aimed at inspiring and supporting the next generation of leaders.

Barack and Michelle also signed a book deal. While Michelle released her memoir, "Becoming", Barack penned "A Promised Land", which details his early life and presidency.

Legacy and Lasting Impact
Barack Obama's presidency is significant for many reasons. As the first Black president, he broke centuries-old barriers and inspired countless people, showing that in America, anything is possible.

His policies and decisions have left a lasting impact, with many debates around them continuing today. Whether one agrees with his politics or not, Obama's ability to inspire, his calm demeanor in crises, and his vision of a united America will always be remembered.

A Symbol of Hope
Barack Obama's journey, from a young boy in Hawaii to the highest office in the land, is a testament to the power of dreams, determination, and resilience. His story reminds us that with belief and effort, barriers can be broken, and change, no matter how daunting, is possible.

1. What inspired Barack Obama to become a community organizer in Chicago?
    - a) A desire to become famous.
    - b) A passion for teaching law.
    - c) Helping people improve their lives, especially in challenging neighborhoods.
    - d) His time at Harvard Law School.

2. What was a central theme of Obama's 2008 presidential campaign?
    - a) Focusing solely on foreign policy.
    - b) Promoting technological advancements.
    - c) Messages of hope and change.
    - d) Establishing a single-party system.

3. Which of the following was NOT a significant moment during Obama's presidency as mentioned in the passage?
    - a) Introduction of a new currency.
    - b) Signing the Paris Climate Accord.
    - d) Reestablishing diplomatic ties with Cuba.

4. In the passage, the term "resilience" most likely means:
    - a) Weakness.
    - b) The ability to recover quickly from difficulties.
    - c) Dependence on others.
    - d) Indecisiveness.

5. How does the author view Barack Obama's presidency?
    - a) Solely as a series of failures.
    - b) As unremarkable and typical.
    - c) As groundbreaking and inspiring, with some challenges.
    - d) As focused only on international affairs.

6. Describe the author's perspective on the significance of Barack Obama's election as the first African American president.

_____
_____
_____
_____

7. Using evidence from the text, explain how Barack Obama's early life experiences influenced his journey and leadership style.

_____
_____
_____
_____

8. What were some of the major accomplishments and initiatives during Barack Obama's presidency?

_____
_____
_____
_____

Analyze the impact of Barack Obama's presidency on the United States. Discuss the key achievements, challenges, and the broader implications of his leadership for the country's future.

_____
_____
_____
_____
_____
_____
_____
_____
_____
_____
_____
_____
_____
_____
_____
_____
_____
_____
_____
_____
_____
_____
_____
_____

Answer key

1. What inspired Barack Obama to become a community organizer in Chicago?
    - a) A desire to become famous.
    - b) A passion for teaching law.
    - <u>c) Helping people improve their lives, especially in challenging neighborhoods.</u>
    - d) His time at Harvard Law School.
2. What was a central theme of Obama's 2008 presidential campaign?
    - a) Focusing solely on foreign policy.
    - b) Promoting technological advancements.
    - <u>c) Messages of hope and change.</u>
    - d) Establishing a single-party system.
3. Which of the following was NOT a significant moment during Obama's presidency as mentioned in the passage?
    - <u>a) Introduction of a new currency.</u>
    - b) Signing the Paris Climate Accord.
    - d) Reestablishing diplomatic ties with Cuba.
4. In the passage, the term "resilience" most likely means:
    - a) Weakness.
    - <u>b) The ability to recover quickly from difficulties.</u>
    - c) Dependence on others.
    - d) Indecisiveness.
5. How does the author view Barack Obama's presidency?
    - a) Solely as a series of failures.
    - b) As unremarkable and typical.
    - <u>c) As groundbreaking and inspiring, with some challenges.</u>
    - d) As focused only on international affairs.

Exit Ticket

HOORAY!

Congratulations! You have read about some of the most influential presidents in American history. Though each president made unique contributions, covering each one in detail was out of the scope of this book. To help you learn a bit more before your exit ticket, we have a list of each president (along with some of their biggest accomplishments) up until the publishing of this book. Feel free to read the list, and/or look online to gather more evidence to answer the questions on the exit ticket. We wish you the best! And we really hope you enjoyed reading our book! If you have any questions or would like to subscribe to our newsletter, please email buddingbrainsbooksllc@gmail.com

United States Presidents

1. George Washington
- Led the Continental Army to victory in the American Revolutionary War.
- Established many key precedents as the first President, including the Cabinet system.
- Oversaw the drafting and ratification of the Bill of Rights.
- Implemented the first Tariff Act (1789) and supported the creation of a national bank.
- Promoted neutrality in foreign affairs, setting a lasting American policy.

2. John Adams
- Played a crucial role in advocating for independence as a diplomat in Europe during the American Revolutionary War.
- As President, avoided war with France, navigating the Quasi-War diplomatically.
- Supported the passage of the Alien and Sedition Acts.
- Helped to establish the U.S. Navy.
- Appointed several federal judges, including Supreme Court Chief Justice John Marshall.

United States Presidents

3. Thomas Jefferson
- Principal author of the Declaration of Independence.
- Made the Louisiana Purchase, doubling the size of the United States.
- Sent the Lewis and Clark expedition to explore the American West.
- Established West Point Military Academy.
- Embargo Act of 1807, an assertive American trade policy.

4. James Madison
- Considered the "Father of the Constitution" for his role in its drafting and promoting the Bill of Rights.
- Led the nation during the War of 1812 against Great Britain.
- Oversaw the creation of the Second Bank of the United States.
- Implemented the Tariff of 1816 to protect American industry.
- Facilitated the American System, promoting strong federal government to manage the economy.

United States Presidents

5. James Monroe
- Introduced the Monroe Doctrine, opposing European colonialism in the Americas.
- Oversaw the Missouri Compromise, balancing power between free and slave states.
- Acquired Florida from Spain with the Adams-Onís Treaty.
- Promoted internal improvements and infrastructure development.
- Era of Good Feelings marked a period of political unity under his presidency.

6. John Quincy Adams
- Negotiated the Adams-Onís Treaty, acquiring Florida and defining the U.S.-Spanish border.
- Formulated the Monroe Doctrine alongside President Monroe.
- Advocated for modernizing the American economy and infrastructure.
- Served as a strong supporter of the National University.
- Championed Native American rights and argued against the Indian Removal Act.

United States Presidents

7. Andrew Jackson
- Founded the Democratic Party and expanded the power of the presidency.
- Responsible for the Indian Removal Act, leading to the Trail of Tears.
- Defeated the British at the Battle of New Orleans in 1815.
- Dismantled the Second Bank of the United States, altering the nation's financial system.
- Supported popular democracy and the extension of voting rights to all white males.

8. Martin Van Buren
- Established an independent federal treasury system.
- Skillfully navigated the Panic of 1837, a major economic crisis.
- Advocated for the "hard money" policy (gold and silver) rather than paper money.
- Played a key role in the formation and establishment of the Democratic Party.
- Managed early diplomatic relations and territorial disputes with Britain.

United States Presidents

9. William Henry Harrison
- First president to die in office, serving the shortest tenure (31 days).
- Renowned for his military leadership, particularly in the Battle of Tippecanoe.
- First president from the Whig Party, marking a shift in political dynamics.
- Utilized his inaugural address to emphasize the importance of strict constructionism and limited federal power.
- His death raised important questions about presidential succession.

10. John Tyler
- Annexed the Republic of Texas, expanding U.S. territory.
- Vetoed bills to create a new national bank, causing a rift in the Whig Party.
- Established the precedent of presidential succession (taking full powers after Harrison's death).
- Supported the Compromise Tariff of 1833 to ease tensions over tariff disputes.
- Signed the Webster-Ashburton Treaty, resolving border issues with Canada.

United States Presidents

11. James K. Polk
- Oversaw the expansion of the U.S. territory by more than one-third through the Oregon Territory settlement and the Mexican-American War.
- Negotiated the Oregon Treaty with Britain, establishing the U.S.-Canada border.
- Signed the Walker Tariff, reducing tariff rates and stimulating trade.
- Established an independent U.S. Treasury System.
- Facilitated the discovery of gold in California, leading to the Gold Rush.

12. Zachary Taylor
- Military leader during the Mexican-American War, earning the nickname "Old Rough and Ready."
- Opposed the spread of slavery into the new territories.
- Supported the admission of California and New Mexico as free states.
- Died suddenly in office, sparking considerable national mourning and political shift.
- Urged the development of a Pacific railroad during his short presidency.

United States Presidents

13. Millard Fillmore
- Completed the Compromise of 1850, which attempted to resolve sectional conflicts over slavery.
- Sent Commodore Perry to Japan, leading to the opening of Japan to the West.
- Enforced the Fugitive Slave Act, causing controversy and deepening the North-South divide.
- Advocated for the modernization of American infrastructure, including railroads and telegraph lines.
- His administration supported trade and diplomatic efforts in Asia and the Pacific.

14. Franklin Pierce
- Signed the Kansas-Nebraska Act, which escalated tensions over slavery.
- Supported the Ostend Manifesto proposing the annexation of Cuba.
- Completed the Gadsden Purchase, adding territory in what is now southern Arizona and New Mexico.
- Supported the development of a transcontinental railroad.
- His administration saw the opening of trade relations with Japan.

United States Presidents

15. James Buchanan
- His administration is often marked by ineffective leadership, particularly in the lead-up to the Civil War.
- Attempted to maintain peace between pro-slavery and anti-slavery factions in the lead-up to the Civil War.
- Supported the Lecompton Constitution, which would have admitted Kansas as a slave state.
- Oversaw the Dred Scott decision, which significantly impacted the political landscape around slavery.
- His inaction and indecision have led many historians to rank him among the least effective Presidents.

16. Abraham Lincoln
- Led the nation through the Civil War, preserving the Union.
- Issued the Emancipation Proclamation, declaring freedom for slaves within the Confederacy.
- Delivered the Gettysburg Address, a defining speech in American history.
- Signed the Homestead Act, providing land for thousands of Americans in the West.
- Established the National Banking System and issued the first federal paper currency.

United States Presidents

17. Andrew Johnson
- First President to be impeached, though he was acquitted by one vote in the Senate.
- Presided over the Reconstruction era following the Civil War.
- Vetoed important civil rights and Reconstruction legislation, which Congress frequently overrode.
- Helped restore Southern states to the Union, though often clashing with Congress over the terms.
- Pardoned thousands of former Confederates through his Reconstruction policies.

18. Ulysses S. Grant
- His administration was pivotal in Reconstruction, working to protect the rights of freed slaves.
- Signed the Civil Rights Act of 1875, guaranteeing African Americans equal treatment in public accommodations, public transportation, and prohibiting exclusion from jury service.
- Supported the Fifteenth Amendment, ensuring voting rights regardless of race.
- Presidency marred by several scandals and corruption, although personally untainted.
- Improved foreign relations and settled claims with Great Britain in the Treaty of Washington.

United States Presidents

19. Rutherford B. Hayes
- Ended Reconstruction by withdrawing federal troops from the South.
- Implemented the first civil service reform laws, including efforts to combat corruption.
- Supported the gold standard against greenback (paper money without gold backing) campaign.
- Promoted education and civil rights for African Americans, though with limited impact.

20. James A. Garfield
- His presidency was cut short by assassination, serving only 200 days.
- Advocated for civil service reform and merit-based government appointments.
- Was a proponent of African American rights, proposing universal education funded by the national government to eliminate racial segregation.
- Sought to reform the Post Office Department and naval appropriations.
- His assassination prompted reforms in the Presidential security and succession laws.

United States Presidents

21. Chester A. Arthur
- Reformed the civil service with the Pendleton Civil Service Reform Act, mandating that government jobs be awarded on merit.
- Oversaw the modernization of the U.S. Navy.
- Advocated for the reduction of tariffs and revision of the tax system.
- Expanded the Navy and improved coastal defenses.

22/24. Grover Cleveland
- Only President to serve two non-consecutive terms.
- Supported the Interstate Commerce Commission and the Dawes Act.
- Vetoed many private pension bills to Civil War veterans whose claims were fraudulent or exaggerated.
- Oversaw the repeal of the Sherman Silver Purchase Act, stabilizing gold reserves.
- Sent federal troops to break the Pullman Strike, enforcing the principle that federal government could intervene when interstate commerce was threatened.

United States Presidents

23. Benjamin Harrison
- Signed the Sherman Antitrust Act, the first legislation to prohibit business monopolies.
- Expanded the U.S. Navy and modernized the military.
- Oversaw the admission of six new states to the Union.
- Supported the McKinley Tariff, which raised duties on foreign goods.
- Signed the landmark Sherman Silver Purchase Act, increasing the coinage of silver but leading to economic controversy.

25. William McKinley
- Led the U.S. to victory in the Spanish-American War, expanding U.S. influence overseas.
- Supported the Gold Standard Act, establishing gold as the sole basis for redeeming paper currency.
- Annexed Hawaii, expanding U.S. territory.
- Promoted high tariffs to protect U.S. industries and workers (McKinley Tariff).
- His assassination brought Theodore Roosevelt to the presidency and shifted the focus towards progressive reforms.

United States Presidents

26. Theodore Roosevelt

- Known for his "Square Deal" domestic policies and conservation efforts, establishing numerous national parks, forests, and monuments.
- Negotiated the end of the Russo-Japanese War, earning the Nobel Peace Prize.
- Supported the construction of the Panama Canal, significantly enhancing global trade routes.
- Established the Pure Food and Drug Act and the Meat Inspection Act, improving food standards and consumer safety.

27. William Howard Taft

- Established the U.S. Chamber of Commerce to address the concerns of business owners.
- Initiated constitutional amendments for a federal income tax (16th Amendment) and the direct election of Senators (17th Amendment).
- Improved the postal system with the introduction of parcel post service.
- Promoted "Dollar Diplomacy" to expand foreign investments and maintain peace.

United States Presidents

28. Woodrow Wilson
- Led the U.S. through World War I, promoting the League of Nations for international peace.
- Established the Federal Reserve System, modernizing the American financial system.
- Implemented the Clayton Antitrust Act to promote fair competition and the Federal Trade Commission to prevent unfair business practices.
- Supported the 19th Amendment, granting women the right to vote.
- Initiated significant progressive reforms including the Federal Farm Loan Act and the Child Labor Reform.

29. Warren G. Harding
- Signed the Fordney-McCumber Tariff, raising American tariffs to protect businesses and farmers.
- Established the Bureau of the Budget, to streamline the process of creating the federal budget.
- Negotiated the Washington Naval Treaty, limiting naval armaments among the major powers.
- Promoted a "return to normalcy" after World War I, focusing on domestic issues and economic growth.

United States Presidents

30. Calvin Coolidge
- Known for his laissez-faire approach to government and economics.
- Maintained policies to reduce the national debt and accumulate a budget surplus.
- Signed the Immigration Act of 1924, severely restricting immigration from certain countries.
- Advocated for civil rights, including the signing of the Indian Citizenship Act, granting full U.S. citizenship to America's Indigenous peoples.
- His tenure saw widespread economic growth, known as the "Roaring Twenties."

31. Herbert Hoover
- His term was predominately marked by the onset of the Great Depression.
- Established the Federal Farm Board to support agricultural prices.
- Implemented the Hoover Dam project, a significant feat in engineering, providing hydroelectric power and flood control.
- Promoted global disarmament and peace through treaties such as the Kellogg-Briand Pact.
- His efforts to combat the Great Depression, including the Smoot-Hawley Tariff and tax increases, were largely viewed as ineffective.

United States Presidents

32. Franklin D. Roosevelt
- Introduced the New Deal programs to recover from the Great Depression, including Social Security and the Works Progress Administration.
- Led the nation during most of World War II, building the Allies coalition and establishing the Lend-Lease program to support them.
- Initiated the establishment of the United Nations.
- Broke tradition by being elected to four terms, leading to the 22nd Amendment, limiting presidential terms.

33. Harry S. Truman
- Made the decision to use atomic bombs against Japan, ending World War II.
- Implemented the Marshall Plan to rebuild Europe after World War II.
- Established the Truman Doctrine to contain communism and the beginning of the Cold War era.
- Oversaw the formation of NATO, a significant military alliance.
- Integrated the Armed Forces by executive order and initiated action towards civil rights.

United States Presidents

34. Dwight D. Eisenhower
- Launched the Interstate Highway System, significantly developing U.S. infrastructure.
- Oversaw an armistice to end the Korean War.
- Established NASA, kickstarting the U.S. space program.
- Promoted the "Atoms for Peace" program, focusing on nuclear nonproliferation.
- Upheld the containment of communism, contributing to the Cold War policy.

35. John F. Kennedy
- Launched the Apollo program, aiming to land a man on the Moon.
- Confronted the Cuban Missile Crisis, one of the Cold War's most tense moments.
- Initiated the Peace Corps to promote world peace and friendship.
- Supported Civil Rights Movement, paving the way for future legislation under his successors.
- Propelled initiatives for mental health and special education through new legislation.

United States Presidents

36. Lyndon B. Johnson
- Signed the Civil Rights Act of 1964 and Voting Rights Act of 1965, landmark achievements in the fight against racial discrimination.
- Implemented the Great Society programs addressing poverty, education, and health care.
- Signed Medicare and Medicaid into law, providing health insurance to the elderly and low-income individuals.
- Advocated for environmental protection, signing several laws to safeguard air and water quality.

37. Richard Nixon
- Established the Environmental Protection Agency (EPA) and signed several major environmental laws.
- Initiated the policy of détente with the Soviet Union and opened diplomatic relations with the People's Republic of China.
- Oversaw the Apollo 11 moon landing, a major milestone in space exploration.
- Implemented the Endangered Species Act, protecting threatened wildlife.
- Resigned from the presidency due to the Watergate scandal, the only U.S. president to do so.

United States Presidents

38. Gerald Ford
- Helped heal the nation after the Watergate scandal and Nixon's resignation by granting Nixon a presidential pardon.
- Faced severe economic challenges, including high inflation and a recession.
- Evacuated nearly 500,000 Americans and South Vietnamese from Vietnam, ending U.S. involvement in the Vietnam War.
- Promoted energy conservation and alternative energy sources during the 1970s energy crisis.

39. Jimmy Carter
- Brokered the historic Camp David Accords between Israel and Egypt, leading to a peace treaty.
- Emphasized human rights in foreign policy.
- Managed the Panama Canal treaties, transferring control of the canal to Panama.
- Faced the Iran hostage crisis, which lasted 444 days and impacted his presidency and legacy.
- Advocated for energy conservation and set the groundwork for sustainable energy policies.

United States Presidents

40. Ronald Reagan
- Known for "Reaganomics," policies focused on tax cuts, deregulation, and control of the money supply to reduce inflation and spur economic growth.
- Played a key role in ending the Cold War, advocating for nuclear disarmament and the Strategic Defense Initiative.
- Survived an assassination attempt, strengthening his popularity.
- Implemented immigration reform and control, granting amnesty to millions of illegal immigrants.
- Appointed the first woman to the Supreme Court, Sandra Day O'Connor.

41. George H. W. Bush
- Led a broad international coalition in the Gulf War, successfully expelling Iraqi forces from Kuwait.
- Signed the Americans with Disabilities Act, a landmark in civil rights for the disabled.
- Oversaw the end of the Cold War and the collapse of the Soviet Union.
- Signed the Clean Air Act Amendments, addressing acid rain, toxic emissions, and ozone depletion.
- Initiated the "Points of Light" movement to promote volunteerism and community service.

United States Presidents

42. Bill Clinton

- Oversaw a period of significant economic growth and budget surpluses.
- Implemented welfare reform, moving from welfare to workfare.
- Signed the North American Free Trade Agreement (NAFTA), expanding trade relationships with Canada and Mexico.
- Led U.S. involvement in NATO interventions in Bosnia and Kosovo, addressing humanitarian crises.
- Became the second U.S. president to be impeached by the House of Representatives, but was acquitted by the Senate.

43. George W. Bush

- Responded to the 9/11 terrorist attacks, initiating the War on Terror, including wars in Afghanistan and Iraq.
- Signed significant tax cuts, the Economic Growth and Tax Relief Reconciliation Act, and the Jobs and Growth Tax Relief Reconciliation Act.
- Established the Department of Homeland Security, enhancing national security efforts.

United States Presidents

44. Barack Obama

- First African American president in U.S. history.
- Signed the Affordable Care Act, significantly reforming healthcare and expanding coverage.
- Authorized the operation that led to the death of Osama bin Laden.
- Negotiated the Iran Nuclear Deal and the Paris Agreement on climate change.

45. Donald Trump

- Implemented tax cuts with the Tax Cuts and Jobs Act, aiming to stimulate economic growth.
- Withdrew the U.S. from the Paris Agreement on climate change and the Iran Nuclear Deal.
- Appointed three Supreme Court justices, significantly shaping the court's composition.
- Faced impeachment twice during his term, acquitted by the Senate both times.

United States Presidents

46. Joe Biden

- Focus on managing the COVID-19 pandemic, including a large-scale vaccination campaign.
- Rejoined the Paris Agreement and recommitted the U.S. to climate change initiatives.
- Signed the American Rescue Plan, aiming to recover the economy impacted by the pandemic.
- Prioritized infrastructure development with the passing of the Infrastructure Investment and Jobs Act.

Think about all of the presidents you have read about. Which three presidents, in your opinion, helped Americans the most? Use evidence from the text to support your answer.

_____
_____
_____
_____
_____
_____
_____
_____
_____
_____
_____
_____
_____
_____
_____
_____
_____
_____
_____
_____
_____

Think about all of the presidents you have read about. Which president's laws or policies affected your life? Use evidence from the text to support your answer.

Think about all of the presidents you have read about. Based on what you have learned, would you run for president? Why or why not? Use evidence from the text to support your answer.

___
___
___
___
___
___
___
___
___
___
___
___
___
___
___
___
___
___
___
___
___
___
___
___
___

Made in the USA
Las Vegas, NV
05 May 2025